C000170917

LIAM WOULFE

Master Cover Letters

Make cover letters easily.

First edition

ISBN: 9798720975708

This book was professionally typeset on Reedsy.
Find out more at reedsy.com

Contents

1

Introduction

You see a new job advertisement and it intrigues you. You look at it in more detail and start to believe that it would be a good fit for you. Maybe it is an exciting new opportunity or maybe it is just more money. Regardless of your reasons you start the application process and then you notice that a cover letter is required. Suddenly you get a sinking feeling as you start to worry about creating your cover letter. You start to wonder why the company wants one, what should you put into your cover letter. Worry sets in and you start to think, should I even bother applying at all? Well, I am here to tell you that it is normal to feel this way. Everyone has felt this way at one time or another, I certainly have.

Cover letters can seem daunting and we all know that a bad one is going to hinder your application. But what if it doesn't have to be like this? What if with some knowledge there was an easy way to create cover letters? Instead of worrying over what you do not have you instead put your skills into practice and create a great cover letter for the job application in question. A cover letter that you are confident in will ensure you get to an interview where you can show off your skills and dazzle the interviewers. If your preferred outcome is to have these skills and this confidence then this is the book for you.

My name is Liam Woulfe and during my career as a manager in a tech-focused SaaS E-Commerce company, I have interviewed thousands of people and I have also read thousands of cover letters. I understand that a cover letter can seem daunting but I want to assure you that they are nothing to be afraid of. I know from both personal and professional experience that it is extremely easy to write a great cover letter when you know what you are doing. I can and will show you what to do in an easy to digest format. I assure you that I will cut out the waffle and keep the business jargon to a bare minimum.

If you want to learn how to master and efficiently construct a great cover letter then I invite you to please read on.

2

What is a Cover Letter and How does it Help you?

Before we get on to how to create a cover letter I find that it helps to first understand what a cover letter is and how it can help you when it is done well. In a nutshell, a cover letter is an introduction as to who you are and why you are suitable for a job that you are applying to. It is also an opportunity for you to make your application noticeable and to grab the hiring manager's attention.

When I am creating a cover letter my aim is to make the hiring manager want to know more about me. I want them to visualize me working in the role. If I can get the hiring manager to view me as part of their team that will pique their interest in me. Once interested in me they are much more likely to push me through to an interview. A great cover letter genuinely helps a lot with this as it tells a hiring manager to look at your application in more detail. A great cover letter will pique the interest of a hiring manager and ensure that you will be moved to the next stage which only increases your opportunity of getting the job.

Ultimately what you want to do is pique the interest of the hiring manager as that vastly increases your chance of moving to the next stage. You must always keep in mind that a cover letter is an introduction to you and also why you will be amazing at the role. I promised no waffle so while I could talk about this for days, let's move on.

3

Why do Companies want a Cover Letter?

Now you know what a cover letter is as far as you the job seeker are concerned. But what are they for hiring managers? For companies? Why do we use them? Why do we ask for them so often?

To understand this I need to share some information on how companies recruit new staff. For general recruitment companies will advertise a role and then applications will occur. What you may not realize is that a role may receive hundreds, thousands if not tens of thousands of applications. This can be quite a lot to process. As a hiring manager, I know what it feels like to sit down and try to read hundreds of applications in a week. It's draining and it becomes really easy to reject someone if their cover letter is poor to average. For me cover letters with the following issues tend to cause an application to be rejected:

- **Obvious common grammar mistakes** – For example not using correct capitalization or paragraph structure
- **Unable to follow basic instruction** - For example not addressing the letter to the required individual as per the job application instructions
- **Generic cover letter** - If you send in a stock generic cover letter it is very

obvious which is not ideal for your application

- **No contact information** – How can we contact you for updates?

Is this fair? Probably not. In a perfect world, every application would be reviewed in full. That means someone spent more than 5 minutes looking at both your cover letter as well as your CV or resume. In reality, this is not always the case and this is what I want to instill in everyone who is reading this. You need to put in the time and effort to create a great cover letter if you want to land that new job.

Now that I have given you some background on recruitment I can tell you that companies want a cover letter as it is an easy way to trim down applications. Most companies have several rounds of tests before a face to face interview. Each test stage is intended to ensure that only the most qualified and likely to be hired individuals get to the face-to-face interview stage. A cover letter is an easy way for companies to cut down on potential interviews as interviews take time and time is money.

Recruiting in general can be quite costly for companies. Even people who are not hired can cost the company money. How might you ask? Well, time is money, every hiring manager who takes the time to read your application, or complete an interview, is factored into the time cost for interviewing. All the time that a hiring manager spends reading your application could have been spent doing any number of other tasks.

Another factor is that there can be(and usually are) recruiters fees and other admin costs associated with hiring new staff. Cover letters help keep costs down as they lead to fewer interviews overall. So while the individual may question why a cover letter is required as most of the information is in your CV or resume, from a company's business perspective it makes sense to want to cut down the potential amount of interviews. The overall aim from the companies perspective is to ensure that only the best fit for their company and role make it through and are potentially hired.

In a nutshell, cover letters are both time and cost-efficient for a company.

4

Generic Cover Letters

There is one extremely bad habit that I have seen countless times in regards to cover letters that I want to address. I mentioned it earlier but it happens enough times that I want to stress it again:

Cover letters need to be customized for each role you are applying to.

This means that you should not create one cover letter and then copy and paste in the company name and role for each separate application. I know this can be frustrating and I know it means more work but in the long term, it is worth it. The main reason I am recommending a customized cover letter for each application is that a generic cover letter is extremely obvious to a hiring manager. For me, whenever I read a generic cover letter it did not instill any confidence that the applicant wanted the role. I get that this is annoying from the applicant's point of view. I have been on both sides of this as both a job seeker and a hiring manager and I do understand the frustration from both sides.

As a job seeker, you are wondering why it's so important when all the details are in your CV or resume anyway. Remember earlier when I said that companies receive tens of thousands of applications? It is entirely possible that no one even looked at your CV or resume which is why it is important to have your great cover letter attached to your application.

As a hiring manager, you spend a considerable amount of your time each week reading applications. While people are professional the simple fact is that everyone is human and people will tend to reject applications that they do not find either interesting or are a fit qualification-wise for the role. If you never mention your skills or qualifications in your cover letter then the hiring manager may not be aware of your skill-set and reject your application.

My advice here is to not gamble, create a customized and great cover letter for each job application.

5

Identifying your Skills

It helps to know what skills you have before you create your cover letter. If you need assistance with this, there is an exercise that I have here which will help you to identify your skills and how to write about them in your cover letters.

To write a great cover letter you need to know what your skill set is. Your skills set is what you bring to the role, what you excel at. Look at your resume or CV and pick out three skills that you believe are your strongest. For example, if you have a qualification for business management you could say that one of your skills is Leadership. Or if you have experience with working for a support team, you could say one of your skills is Communication. Or you are a qualified software developer you could say one of your skills is your attention to detail. As another example, maybe you have a hobby of coaching a local sports team and you could say that one of your skills is your organizational ability.

If you are still unsure of how to identify your skills, just look at your qualifications, your achievements and think about how you succeeded at them or what skills you gained from completing them. If you still can't think of any, search for your qualifications in a web browser and look at what skill set is expected for each role. This can be useful to remind us what skills we use. Once you have an idea of what to do, write these skills down in a list and write a one-line sentence about why you are good at this skill. Just write what comes to mind, it does not have to be phrased perfectly as long as it makes sense to you.

For example, using the skills above our sample list might look like this:

- **Leadership** – I have successfully managed several teams in my career
- **Communication** - I am skilled in dealing with difficult customer situations
- **Attention to Detail** – I ensure that my work is correct the first time
- **Organizational Ability** - I am skilled at ensuring training and meetings occur on time every week

Now you know what your skills are and why you are good at each one. These are your selling points that you will use in your cover letters. When you already know what you are great at, which are your selling points, you already have the main points you want to include in your cover letter. Once you have this information and more critically, are aware of it, it will help you to craft great cover letters. This is why I recommend to everyone to complete this at least once as it will be useful when you are creating your cover letters.

6

How to Structure a Cover Letter

How to Structure a Cover Letter

Ok so now we know what a cover letter is, why it helps you and why companies require them so often. Now we are going to learn how you structure a cover letter. I have a template that you can use that is attached to this lesson but study the material first so that the template makes sense. I want you to succeed and I want you to know what you are doing, so learn first and then put what you have learned into practice.

Cover letters should have the following elements:

Dear Person I am applying to
   Generally speaking, job applications will tell you who to direct a cover letter to. Please use this name - if you do not it is a red flag. Why is it a red flag? Well, it means that you are unable to follow basic instructions. If you are unable to follow basic instruction it will likely count against you. If there is no name provided the expected behavior is to use *"To whom it may concern"*

Brief Intro

In this section, you say who you are and mention the job that you are applying for. For example:

"My name is John and I am applying for the Technical Customer Support role that you have advertised."

Paragraph 1

Next is your Paragraph where you mention relevant skills, qualifications and/or achievements from your CV or resume that show why you are a good fit for the job. Remember your skills from earlier? Use the relevant ones to create this section. When you are adding them, talk about your skills as if you were speaking to the hiring manager in person. This will help you write a more conversational easily flowing cover letter and it will make you more personable, which is only a good thing.

Closing Paragraph

Your closing paragraph needs to summarize why you are the best candidate for the job and also expressing your desire for it. Are you passionate about the industry due to your hobbies? Then mention it in this section. Have you experience with a specific aspect of this role? Mention it here. If you are applying for a company that aligns to your values and beliefs, this would be a good place to mention this also.

Tailing Sentence

Keep this simple and straightforward. I prefer to use *"I look forward to hearing from you"* as it is a positive way to end. It also implies that you will be hearing back from the company as your application is good enough to get to the next stage. Remember to project confidence.

Signature

Finally, add a closing with either a *"Thanks"* or a *"Regards"* and sign under it as you would a normal letter. I prefer to use thanks but feel free to use what you feel fits best for your application. Under your signature put in your name, address, phone number and email address. If you have a LinkedIn profile this is also a good place to add this.

7

Advice

Now you know how to structure your cover letter and what kind of information to put into each section. So far this is pretty awesome. In this section I want to share advice and what to do, and not do, to ensure your cover letter is great. If you take nothing else away from this book, please take this advice on board as it will assist you with creating a great cover letter for your job applications.

Keep it professional

Personal touches are fine as long as it stays professional. Please remember that you are sending this cover letter to a company. Whatever you send may end up being saved on a database for several years depending on the laws in the company's country. Please do not put anything into your cover letter that you would not mind anyone reading. Also remember to stay polite throughout the cover letter.

Use correct grammar

Nothing is more off-putting than incorrect grammar. I would recommend that you use a site like Grammarly which will help you ensure that your grammar is correct. At the time of this book being created, Grammarly is free and it has a chrome extension that makes it even easier to use. As a caveat to this, no one will expect you to be perfectly correct but if you are not using commas, capitalization, paragraph structure, etc., it is a red flag and it will count against you so do yourself a favor and double-check your grammar

Research the company

It never hurts to include specific details on the company you are applying to. Not sure on how to find this out? Read the company's website as well as their social media. If there is anything on there that you can relate to in a positive or meaningful way try and include it in some way in your cover letter.

For example, if the company has recently expanded into France and you speak French, you could mention this in your cover letter as it would be another skill that would be beneficial to the company that you have. Even if the role you are applying for does not have a french speaking requirement, mention your skill as it makes you a more valuable hire which is only good for you.

Humanize yourself

This is optional but it can be a good idea to humanize yourself to the hiring manager. As I mentioned earlier, hiring managers tend to read thousands of cover letters a week. If you can add anything that is personal yet still professional, that will make your letter stand out or better yet be memorable which is only a good thing.

For example, you could mention relevant hobbies. Maybe you are applying for a graphical artist role and you mention that you also love painting miniatures in your spare time. You could talk about how this gives you a deeper understanding of color and you feel that this skill translates over into your day job.

Maybe you are applying for a technical support role and you also have a hobby where you build and maintain a private gaming server. You could mention how this helps you in your day job as it gives you technical support experience due to server updates or issues as well as customer support experience from dealing with users of your server.

As another example, if you are studying for a new qualification and it is relevant for the job application you could mention it also. For example, if the job is for a Technical Customer Support specialist and you are studying to learn SQL, which is a programming language used for databases, mention it as this shows that you are technically minded and looking to improve your skill set. These are huge plus points for a potential employer.

These are just some examples, be creative, look at what your hobbies are and think how could or do they help you in your skill-set in relation to this job?

Overall if you decide to add in anything like this (remember it is optional and likely will be extremely dependent on the job itself), be imaginative and add it in like you are having a conversation with the person reading the cover letter.

Honesty

If you add something you don't do or know anything about, it will likely come up again, and being dishonest is a big no-no to being hired. Everyone exaggerates, hiring managers to know this. But there is a difference between exaggerating and outright lying. Personally, whenever I caught someone in an outright lie, for example claiming they had a qualification they did not, they were not hired. Don't make that mistake.

Be confident bordering on arrogant

When I am writing a cover letter, this is the part that I used to have the most trouble with. Why might you ask? Well I am from Ireland. This may be surprising but we tend to not be all that confident culturally by nature and hence I am not a naturally confident person. I had to learn my confidence. If I can learn it then you can too. Trust me. I could write an entire book about how to gain confidence and someday I might but right now I know that it can be a daunting prospect to project self confidence.

You need to keep telling yourself that you are the best candidate for this role due to your skills, your qualifications and your achievements. A well written and confident cover letter will convince even your worst critic that you should get through to an interview so you can impress the hiring manager with your skills, experience and personality. The attitude you want to convey in your cover letter is:

"I am the best, you need to hire me as I am the best and only choice, choosing someone else would not be a good choice".

I would not phrase it exactly this way but this is the sentiment you want to get across in your cover letter.

Keep it as brief as possible

It is possible to fall into the trap of writing walls of text describing everything about you and why you are so amazing. This is a mistake. You need to be brief and to the point. Your CV or resume has more specific details. Do not put off a hiring manager by waffling on for pages and pages as they will lose interest. A good rule of thumb is to keep your cover letter to one page at the very most.

Do not include political or religious views

It is fine having strong views on either of these topics but please do not put them in a cover letter. You are entitled to your views, I am not saying you are not. But they have no place in a cover letter for a job application. This is a simple fact. If you do include these views, regardless of what they are or if the hiring manager agrees with you (or not), the simple fact is that it is a huge red flag for a hiring manager if you include these views in a cover letter. Honestly if you include views like this it will likely lead to your application failing.

No hiring manager I know, and I include myself in this, would be comfortable having someone on their team that would freely express any views on topics such as these without knowing who they are speaking to. You are entitled to your opinion whatever it may be. No one is questioning that. For your application's sake please leave it out of your cover letter as 99.9% of the time it will only hurt your application.

8

Cover Letter Template

Here is a template that I recommend you use to structure your cover letters.

Title: Application for [Title of Role on Job Advertisement]

[RECIPIENT NAME]
[RECIPIENT'S COMPANY]
[RECIPIENT'S ADDRESS]
[DATE]

Dear [Person/Company you are applying to]

[Brief Intro]

[Paragraph 1]

[Closing Paragraph]

[Tailing Sentence]

[Signature:]

COVER LETTER TEMPLATE

[Your name]
[Your address]
[Your phone number]
[Your email address]
[Linkedin URL]

9

Frequently Asked Questions

Should I save all my cover letters?

Yes absolutely. I would recommend that you keep a record of all correspondence that you send to a company. The advantage of keeping your cover letters is that while you should create a new cover letter and tailor it for each job application, you can re-use specific phrases and descriptions if you are happy with how they read and if they are a fit. I admit this will only come with experience but there is no harm in keeping your past cover letters for reference.

Is proofreading important?

This is another hard yes. As I mentioned previously grammar is important. So is sentence structure. Make sure you double check everything in your cover letter - you don't want to make the mistake of a typo ruining all of your time and effort.

If I am emailing my cover letter does the file format matter?

Generally I would recommend .PDF as it will retain the formatting correctly. However .doc is also fine. Generally speaking it will say in the job application, or description, what format the file needs to be. I would highly recommend using whatever your new employer has requested.

Can I add in volunteer work?

Absolutely, employers love it when their employees do volunteer work in the community. If this is something you are already doing and you are passionate about it mention it in your cover letter. A sentence or two should be fine.

Can I name drop a mutual contact?

You can but I would advise caution on how you phrase it. I would also highly recommend that you get the OK from your mutual contact before you put their name in your letter. For example if you were to add in:

"Your Customer Support Manager Mary who is a friend of mine spoke to me about this role and suggested I apply."

This is fine as it shows that your friend sought you out and made a direct call to action for you to apply. In this situation it would be normal for the hiring manager to ask Mary about you and your application. This will give Mary an opportunity to talk positively about you, which is only a good thing for you.

However if you were to add in:

"I know your Customer Support Manager Mary, we went to school together. We worked well there so I think we would be a good fit at your company".

This is not very good as it simply states that you know Mary from school and you both worked together well in your opinion. If Mary does not know about this and is asked about you, the likely response the hiring manager will get is confusion which does not help you.

Name dropping can be helpful but only if it is relevant and OKed by your mutual contact. As a side point you may also see this referred to as a referral cover letter. From my experiences referrals were always submitted by the mutual contact rather than the applicant (that's you!) specifically though you would still create the cover letter, there just wouldn't be a mention of the mutual contact in it.

I hear the term USP a lot in regards to cover letters. What is this?

USP stands for Unique Selling Proposition which is an advertising term and honestly it is just a slightly fancy way of saying what I covered in the Identifying your skills as well as the *What is a Cover Letter and how does it help you?* chapters. I did not mention the term specifically as I want to cut out jargon, not add more in.

Can I use bullet points?

Sure, absolutely if used correctly. Bullet points should be used to convey quick pieces of information that are more easily read in a list form. Do not create your entire cover letter in bullet point form though.

Do I put references in a cover letter?

No, these will come up later, likely in your interview or pre-interview. Do not put them in your cover letter. If you do they will get glossed over and look like needless filler.

Should I send a thank you letter?

If you went to an interview then you can if you prefer. If you didn't I wouldn't go to the effort as you would be essentially just thanking someone for reading your letter which seems a bit odd to me. Why waste everyone's time if they are not interested in you.

Can I use a fancy font?

No, don't. Cover letters are professional formal documents and should be treated as such. Do not use a fancy looking font. I would recommend using Times New Roman, Arial, Lato or Roboto. These are all very similar and are accepted formal industry fonts.

The job application doesn't ask for a cover letter, should I send one?

It can't hurt to still send one and after reading this book you will be able to create a great one. My advice would be to put what you have learned into practice and send one in anyway. It may even help you stand out from the crowd which is only a good thing.

Can I include a picture?

No, do not put in any picture in your cover letter. Especially if it is a picture of you. If an employer asks for a picture of you in a job application it is highly likely that they are breaking the law, though this is dependent on where you are in the world.

Can I include an image or meme?

No. This is a formal document and images should not be included. I have seen people trying to add memes and other images to cover letters and I want to assure you that it is not a particularly good idea to do so. Do yourself a favor and just avoid this by leaving it out and keeping it professional.

What about buzzwords, can or should I include them?

I would not really recommend it. While you want to be professional in a cover letter, you also want to be yourself, within reason. Hiring managers want to be interested in you. If you use lots of buzzwords we tend to roll our eyes as we have seen it countless times before. As a caveat to this, if you are applying for a role that tends to use a lot of buzzwords, such as HR or Management, I can understand that you may want to use them. Just understand what they mean and be ready to talk about them.

There is no point mentioning that you promote synergy if you do not know what it is, for example. If you decide to use buzzwords, be prepared to back them up when you get to an interview.

I am highly skilled and I want to include all my skills, can I?

I wouldn't recommend it. Pick out your top 3 to 4 and use those. Highlight what you are best at. You can mention the rest in your interview.

Can I follow up on my cover letter?

This question is a little off topic for this book but I understand that you may still be thinking about it. You can but I would wait at least 10 working days at a minimum. I would advise caution about this though as you want to seem eager while not overly pushy which is a delicate balancing act.

Should I include keywords from the job description to bypass applicant tracking systems?

I get asked about this a lot. Honestly any company I ever worked at did not use an applicant auto scan system. Yes that means that every single application was read in person and honestly I preferred that. But I know it's used in other companies. My advice on this is to simply include, if you can, as many of the keywords that the job description mentions on your cover letter.

Why didn't you give example cover letters in this book?

I want you all to be able to create cover letters about you using the skills and knowledge you have attained in this book. I don't want you to copy and edit an example I provided as you won't learn the skills as well as you would have if you created it on your own. I want you all to succeed and from my experiences I believe this is the best way for this to occur.

Should I include my qualification subject results?

No as it is not needed. Hiring managers want to know if you are qualified, we do not really care what result you got on your individual subjects, we just want to know if you are qualified to do the role or not.

10

Practice, Practice, Practice

As with any skill you will improve over time as long as you continue to practice it. Take what you have learned from this book, look at a job application that you would love to get and write out a cover letter based on it. Remember to use everything that you have learned so far. Practice, as with everything, makes perfect.

If by now you are not yet motivated or confident enough I want to share some advice that one of my mentors shared with me that has helped me a lot in my life. It is that at one point every expert knew nothing about their subject matter. Everyone has to start somewhere. The fact that you picked up this book shows that you want to improve. Believe in yourself. You can do this.

11

Conclusion

As a final piece of advice I would tell you that cover letters do not need to be stressful. I know they can be daunting. Just remember to be confident and sell your skill set as best you can. You have the qualifications and achievements and if you stick to the skills you learned here, you can do this.

I want to take this opportunity to wish everyone who has taken the time to read this the very best fortune for your job applications and thank you for reading this book. I hope you have enjoyed it and that you found something useful here that will help you in some meaningful way.

If you found this book useful, please consider leaving a short review on Amazon.

Also if you enjoyed this content and want to see more of my work, you can find me at www.wyn.ie Please come by and say hi.

Finally I want to wish you the very best. Stay safe.

About the Author

Liam Woulfe can usually be found brainstorming a new course or writing a new book. Coming from a career focused on managing top performing technical support teams across four continents for companies on the Fortune 500 list, Liam has quite a bit to share. Couple this with an eagerness for helping people, Liam strives to share what he has learned in his career with the world.

Liam believes everyone should achieve the success they deserve and recognizes that sometimes we all need a helping hand. As the founder of WYN, an Irish based E-Learning provider, Liam works every day to achieve this dream. Liam manages all this from his home in Limerick which he shares with his family.

If anyone would like to get in touch with Liam you can do so from www.wyn.ie or by emailing contact@wyn.ie

"Lets WYN together"